SURVIVING
DYSFUNCTION

It's Not Normal But My Reality

Olivia B. Grace

SURVIVING DYSFUNCTION. Copyright © 2020 by Olivia B. Grace.

All rights reserved. Printed in the United States of America. No part of this book may be used or reproduced in any manner whatsoever without written permission, except in the case of brief quotations embodied in critical articles or reviews.

Publishing Services by Lynda D. Mallory.
See www.lyndadmallory.com

All Scriptures, unless otherwise stated, are taken from the Holy Bible, New King James Version Copyright © 1982 by Thomas Nelson, Inc. Used by permission. All rights reserved. Bible used was the Holy Bible NKJV, Nashville: Thomas Nelson, 1994.

ISBN: 978-0-578-76733-8 *(paperback)*
978-0-578-82142-9 *(eBook)*

Printed in the United States of America

This book is dedicated to my parents, and to my husband, children, and grandchildren. To my family, thank you so much for your love and support.

Table of Contents

INTRODUCTION 7

CHAPTER 1 11

CHAPTER 2 13

CHAPTER 3 19

CHAPTER 4 25

CHAPTER 5 27

CHAPTER 6 29

CHAPTER 7 31

CHAPTER 8 35

CHAPTER 9 37

CHAPTER 10 39

CHAPTER 11 41

CHAPTER 12 43

CONCLUSION 45

INTRODUCTION

Someone once said to me the relationship that I have with my sister is not normal, and to that I say, it may not look normal to you from the outside looking in. But, it's quite normal to me. I've been dealing with dysfunction in my family for so long, it's just my way of life. I am not going to act like it's okay, because it is not okay. What I have gone through with my sister is definitely not normal, but it is my story, and my reality. I have accepted the fact that we are a dysfunctional family. I've also learned to move on from all of the drama. As difficult as it has been, I had to move on beyond this for my own piece of mind.

My sister also doesn't have a good relationship with my mother. I think my parents let her get away with so much bad behavior over the years, that it just became Zoe's way of life. Zoe was so used to having her way with them, that when she didn't get her way, it was traumatic for her. And traumatic, might be an understatement.

I'm sure having a child with mental health issues is a tough pill to swallow for some parents. For whatever reason, or let's say for reasons unknown, my parents decided to sweep Zoe's erratic behavior under the rug and let it fester. The rage that is embedded in Zoe runs deep. I've seen that rage up close and personal and it's hard to watch. She even calls me by another name when her other personality comes out. I hope that she is and continues to get help for her behavioral and anger management issues, but I guess you first have to acknowledge that you have a problem; for which she hasn't to my knowledge.

Some of you may be wondering why I am writing this book. I am writing this book because I have witnessed and dealt with a lot over the years, as it relates to Zoe's destructive behavior. I started keeping notes on Zoe's behavior years ago. Don't ask me why, but I just did. The strain that her behavioral issues have put on my family is unbelievable. I did not realize how long I had been keeping notes on her behavior until recently. Believe me, I know every family has its problems, but this is my life. And, in case you are wondering about me and how this has affected me, I am good. I am blessed. I survived the dysfunction.

Unfortunately, at the time of this writing, I had to deal with another episode of Zoe's behavior. Mom was sick and quite frail in the hospital. In the end, mom's health and safety was not compromised, and that is all that matters.

So, if this book can help one person to love themselves regardless of the pain they endure from within their family, then I will have accomplished my goal!

Surviving Dysfunction:
It's Not Normal But My Reality
CHAPTER I

As I think back over the last fifteen years or so, it's clear to me that Zoe has some animosity towards my mother. That's not to say that she doesn't love her, but I've seen how she treats mom and let's just say it's not normal, but something that I've witnessed time and time again. I don't think you can treat your mother the way Zoe has, without there being some hostility there. It's like Zoe had a chip on her shoulders, as it relates to mom.

When I was younger, I saw Zoe disrespect mom in front of other family members. We were at my grandmother's house. I don't remember if it was a cookout or we were just eating outside, but I remember other family members being there and witnessed this behavior from Zoe. I remember thinking, why is she talking to mom that way? And, why didn't someone stop her? I also remember some drama around Zoe's wedding. I remember mom feeling like she wasn't welcome at the wedding. There was some friction between mom and Zoe. But, my parents put on a smile and went anyway because they wanted to be there for Zoe, no matter what.

As Zoe's sister, I know what it feels like to be envied by her so much that when she is speaking or saying something that is meant specifically for me to hear, she doesn't speak directly to me. She talks to me, through other family members, mainly mom. I have to say, it's rather strange. Some would say that is not normal, but I say it's my normal. You see, I'm there in the room, but at the same time it feels like I'm not. It's like one of those outer body experiences. Even after I speak up and say, "I'm here, you can talk directly to me", she still does not acknowledge me. She chooses to ignore me because in her mind, I'm in the way of her agenda.

Zoe was the baby of the family before I was born. I was told she was hoping for a baby brother when I came along, but God had other plans. I became the baby of the family that day; for which Zoe still struggles with today.

Was it sibling rivalry or just family drama? Or, was it a much bigger issue: one that I had no control over? It took me a while to figure that out.

Surviving Dysfunction:
It's Not Normal But My Reality
CHAPTER 2

During the time of my brother's death, Zoe sided with someone outside of the family, Hannah, and not with us. That's right, Zoe split from the family and tore us apart when we should have been united. One issue was, and there were many, my brother wanted a small memorial service and not a large funeral at the time of death, but Zoe and Hannah did all they could to go against his wishes. He had lost a lot of weight, due to his illness and made his wishes quite known. This was a travesty for my family and the aftershocks still live today.

Zoe also had family members, outside of our circle, involved in our business during this time. She had them trying to tell us what my brother wanted. When Zoe felt like she wasn't getting her way with us, that's what she'd do, go outside of our circle to get her way. While we knew him best, here they were trying to tell us how to funeralize our loved one. And, why? Why, because of Zoe. It was hard to believe that we were going through this while we were grieving for my brother, but Zoe made it all about Zoe. We didn't matter to her during this time.

My brother was not married at the time of death, so mom was in charge of everything, but Zoe decided to take over since she felt it was what my brother wanted her to do. Of course that was only in her mind, and was a bad decision on her part, because it was a mess and so not worth it for the family. At the time, I felt like we let him down, or should I say, she let him down. His daughter disconnected from the family, but I am told she is doing well. Maybe one day she will re-connect with the family. In addition, we almost lost his son due to Zoe's behavior and betrayal.

And, the betrayal didn't stop there! Zoe and another family member removed my husband from the list of names to ride in the family car to my brother's funeral, since he was an honorary pallbearer. And, yes you read it right honorary, which required no action on his part. Their rationale for this decision made no sense and was so insensitive. My first thought was, they had to know better. I later heard that my cousin was leading the pack and saying that my husband was not "immediate" family, and therefore did not need to ride in the family car. And, you guessed it, Zoe went right along with it and did not stand up for me or my husband because she was too busy making room for Hannah in the family car. *Maybe it was her inner voice telling her that she had to go against me, since she sees everything as a competition between us?* What I do know is, it was so wrong on all levels.

I didn't find out about my husband being removed from the list until the morning of the funeral when I looked at the list of names of who were riding in the family car. I was shocked that Zoe didn't discuss this with me before then, as her sister, but I learned later that's how she operates. She likes the element of surprise, hoping that she can just throw it at you at the last minute, in hopes of getting her way. I was so upset, and was already hurting from losing my brother. My aunt kept telling me, "don't say anything now, it's not the time." Emotions were extra high that day for me. I know, it's not normal, but my reality. Zoe's main concern was appeasing Hannah; not that I, her sister, should have my husband by my side on the day of my brother's funeral.

At the time, I could not understand it. Why would she do that? Family should not treat family like this. *That inner voice of hers took over.* And, as time went on, I started to wonder. Was it because Zoe was no longer married and maybe she was resentful of me because I was married? Why not just be happy for me? But, it was that competition thing, that's in her mind, as it relates to me.

She also felt that she had a closer relationship with my brother than "anyone" else during this time, but that was just in her mind too. We all loved my brother and we were all grieving for him. My husband loved my brother just like his own brother and he didn't deserve to be treated like that because of her jealousy for me. Again, just like before, years ago, my question was why didn't someone stop her? But it was their little plan, Zoe, my cousin, and Hannah. They knew exactly what they were doing, but it didn't matter to them at the time. It was a debacle for the family. It was like a double whammy. We were grieving for my brother, but then we had to deal with all of Zoe's deceit and backstabbing. And, it definitely wasn't what my brother wanted. He was the one that kept us all together. So, all of the drama and betrayal was disrespectful to his legacy and to the family. I decided after all of that, I would never let something like this happen again, when we are grieving for a loved one. We would work together in unity, the way it should be, and that is what we have done.

You see, my brother was the only one that Zoe listened to. She didn't listen to my mother or my father. So, there was no one to reel her in and tell her right from wrong, since he was gone. There was no one there to tell her that blood is thicker than water or that you do not desert your family when you lose a loved one. And, you know she didn't listen to me during this time. I was just wasting my breath. For her, it was all about winning and having things done her way. In her mind, we were on opposite sides of the fence, so why would she want to sit down with me and work things out during this time? She knew what she was doing was wrong, but why didn't it matter? It didn't matter because her feelings about me that are buried so deep within, took over. This was not normal. Believe me, I know, but my reality.

As Zoe continued working against us during this time, I did everything that I could to try to keep the family together, but Zoe did so much damage to the family there are relationships that will never be restored. We were betrayed by one of our own, and to this day, she has never apologized to mom, dad, me or anyone else in the family for her deceitful behavior during such a difficult time for us. And, why would she? In her mind, she did nothing wrong. She never does anything wrong. It's always someone else's fault. She has made me out to be the bad sister to her confidants. Some of those confidants just happen to be family members, so that's put a whole other spin on things. As for me, I just keep my head up and treat them with respect. And, those who really know me, know better anyway. They know Zoe has some serious issues, and it's not anything that I have done to her. I was born. That's her issue with me.

Surviving Dysfunction:
It's Not Normal But My Reality
CHAPTER 3

When dad decided to retire and come home to care for my mom, we threw him a party after Thanksgiving that year. I had put in a lot of time and effort to ensure the party went over well. Zoe likes to take credit when a "good" plan comes together, but wants none of the responsibility to go along with it. In other words, she did not want to do any of the work for this event, and tried her best to throw a wrench into the party plans by deciding, if she didn't speak first at the event then she wasn't going to show up. She also had issues with the musical group that was singing, and demanded changes, just a few days before the party, on the holiday. She said the group would sound better acapella, if they sang on an empty stomach, so she demanded that they sing before they eat. The plans already in place were they would eat first and then sing, as they usually do, I might add. She really took issue with this. And I mean really!

Zoe waited until after our Thanksgiving dinner, to bring all this up to us. It was probably on her mind all through dinner. I think that was her plan to wait until we had our Thanksgiving dinner and then spring it on us. Well, mom didn't make any changes to the party that Zoe wanted. I'll just say it was a long night that night after she didn't get her way, and that's when I saw another side of Zoe; her other personality. That evening did not end well, and that's the first time that I heard her call me by another name. And, she used that name for me over and over that night. I will never forget what she called me that night. In addition, she tried to get dad to pick sides that night; her or me. Nothing new, that's how she usually operated. She also tried to make him feel guilty because she felt like I had won. Won what? There is no competition between us; only in her mind.

Thinking back, she did the same thing with mom. If Zoe didn't get her way, she would put mom in the middle and try to make mom side with her over me. I realized that it was much bigger than sibling rivalry that night. She displayed so much hostility toward me that night. Her anger is so deeply rooted, as it relates to me. Don't get me wrong, I had seen this behavior on display before, but that night I saw it on a whole other level. I always knew Zoe had behavior issues. She had a short temper and would become extremely angry when she did not get her way. However, that night, I realized that Zoe was really suffering from something; and it was much bigger than me or any of us. We ended up calling the police that night, and mom and dad's safety quickly became my major concern. I realized that I had to take care of them and be there for them. They were elderly and fragile and needed to be protected; no matter who it was.

We planned a beautiful party for dad, but Zoe decided she would overshadow the event by not coming. But, it was a lovely affair, and dad enjoyed his party. Zoe did hurt my parents by not showing up. They were disappointed and I think it actually broke mom's spirit over time, and took a toll on her mentally. Zoe never called them to say why she didn't come to the party, and she didn't even answer their calls or return their calls when they tried to reach out to her, for four months. They were worried sick for her. The family was concerned for Zoe given what we had witnessed before the event. My mom took it the worst. I saw her pain up close and personal. But, this was a pattern for Zoe -- hurting her family and never apologizing for it.

Zoe had several friends and confidants that knew she wasn't well during this time and knew she suffered from depression, but all I heard from them was excuses for her behavior. Such as, "she just needs time, or she will come around"; even after we said she was aggressive with dad on that night. This definitely was not normal, but quickly became our reality. Her friends also knew that she was jealous of me, and that everything was a competition between us, in Zoe's mind. One of her friends really didn't want to talk to me about Zoe's behavior and said, "if Zoe finds out we are talking, she's going to be upset." Really? I mean Zoe was struggling, and that was all she could say. I was expecting more from her. And, the tone in her voice made me quickly realize that she was more concerned with preserving their friendship, rather than being honest with Zoe. She even attempted to belittle my dad's party, all because Zoe made a choice not to be there. How dare she? I guess she made Zoe proud that day. Let's just say I moved on. Misery loves company and I did not have time for that.

    The family did offer Zoe an olive branch to get some help, but she was in denial and chose to play the victim; that familiar role for her. Instead of coming to the family and addressing this issue privately and in unity, she chose to tell other family members and friends that it was our entire fault that she chose not to come to the party. No one or "anything" should have stopped her from coming to his party; as long as she was still breathing. I think you get my point, but playing the victim worked for her for many years, so why would she stop now? After this incident, she kept her distance from the family, and she never discussed the party with me. It took her eight or nine months before she even came to see my parents again.

In spite of all of Zoe's efforts, dad loved his party. That is all he talked about for the longest time. The rest of us loved the party too and spoke of it often; as well as the big smile on dad's face. I will never forget that party and the joy that it brought him. There is something else that I will never forget, and that is what we saw and experienced with Zoe, all because she did not get her way. It is not normal, but my reality.

Surviving Dysfunction:

It's Not Normal But My Reality

CHAPTER 4

It was a tough holiday season for mom that year. Zoe hadn't called my parents or come to see them, and she didn't come to Christmas dinner at their house. This actually became a pattern of hers because she was a no show for the next Christmas as well. Zoe's gift from last Christmas was under the tree again. Mom put it back under the Christmas tree hoping she would come, and she didn't. This was heartbreaking for mom. She really struggled with this. Dad seemed to be handling it better, but the silence was heart wrenching for mom. Not being able to reach her own child, when she knew her child needed help. I saw her pain, I heard her pain, and I felt her pain. No mother should have to endure such pain.

While I realize this may happen in other families, I am talking about my mother and how I lived through this pain with her. Zoe never spent another Thanksgiving, Christmas, or birthday dinner with my parents or the rest of us after that. As a unit, we accepted that and moved on. The saying around our house growing up was, "you don't let one monkey stop the show." We moved on and continued to make sure that my parents celebrated every holiday and birthday with lots of love from their family, in spite of Zoe's absence.

I used to ask, what happened? Why are we so different? Mom and dad raised us to respect one another and to treat others the way we wanted to be treated. Why the jealousy now that we are adults? Isn't that something that you are supposed to grow out of? The bible says, when we grow up, we should lose our childish ways. We were both taught to honor our mother and father. We both went to church and Sunday school, and vacation bible school, during the summer. I knew that I could never purposefully hurt my parents like that. As time went on, I stopped wondering about Zoe's behavior after I realized God's purpose for me, and that was to care for mom and dad, and to be there for them for whatever they needed.

Surviving Dysfunction:
It's Not Normal But My Reality
CHAPTER 5

As mom's health declined, along with the additional stress she endured from Zoe, we got aides to assist with her health care.

Dad used to tell one of the aides, Maggie, that if it wasn't for me, they would probably be in the street somewhere. She said he would often make that statement since he knew he could not depend on Zoe to help with them. Maggie told me this after my dad passed away. Maggie was there several days a week and witnessed many conversations in their house. Dad was a very private person, but trusted her and would confide in her from time to time. Maggie overheard many phone calls with dad and Zoe when he would try to get her to help with them for doctor's appointments and other things. She said all my dad got was excuses. Zoe did not want to commit to help care for them. Maggie said while dad was disappointed, he never let it get him down. He knew he could depend on my family and me for anything. On the other hand, mom struggled with Zoe's choice not to help with them when they were always there for her.

They say the roles reverse as your parents' age, you are supposed to give back and care for them, and that is what my family and I did. We stopped by to check on them and to make sure they had food to eat on a regular basis. We did the grocery shopping; we made sure they got to their doctor's appointments; and assisted with their finances. We did whatever they needed. As mentioned earlier, we made sure they still had a Thanksgiving and a Christmas each year. We had family dinners at their house, my house, or my daughter's house. We made sure they still had birthday and anniversary celebrations. I personally made sure that we acknowledged them on Valentine's Day, since it is one of my favorite holidays. We worked hard to ensure that they had a normal family life. They deserved that and more. We did our best to keep them happy.

Surviving Dysfunction:

It's Not Normal, But My Reality

CHAPTER 6

Just as dad could not get Zoe to help with them, when I asked her to help, it was like pulling teeth. I know, no surprise right! Every time I would call her, it was pretty much the same thing, excuses. I remember one time I was trying to set up a schedule on a calendar for everyone to pick a day or an evening they could stop by the house and check in on mom and dad or fix dinner for them, so we all would not be there at the same time. I was trying to be organized in hopes of making sure mom and dad were covered, since they were living alone and were both elderly.

Well, Zoe would not commit to anything and lost her temper. She told me not to depend on her! She said, "I'm sorry, but I have to do blah, blah, blah." It did not sound like an apology to me then or whenever she said it. I finally stopped asking her to help with them for my own piece of mind. It took me awhile to get to that point, but I came to realize that she was not going to do her share no matter how many times or ways I asked her. In Zoe's mind, if she assisted with caring for her own parents, then she was helping me out, and she did not want to do that. Think about that for a minute. Your parents are still alive and kicking, but you do not want to help with them, because in your mind, you are helping your sister and you cannot do that because of your negative feelings toward her.

After that, I only asked family members or friends that I knew I could depend on, to help with mom and dad. *Tranquility.*

Surviving Dysfunction:
It's Not Normal But My Reality
CHAPTER 7

Close to a year after my dad's party, Zoe started coming back around and staying at my parents' house again; off and on. A few days before this Christmas, mom started talking to me about how Zoe mistreated her and the nasty way that she talked to her. Mom started to cry. She could see that Zoe was not well. Mom said that no child should speak to its mother the way that Zoe talks to her. Mom said one little word would set her off. Mom would try to talk to Zoe about what happened last Christmas when she did not hear from Zoe or see her on Christmas day. She asked Zoe if Christmas was going to be better this year. Zoe did not want to hear about it, stormed off, and walked away from mom. It was a very difficult time for mom. She knew that her child was not well but she could not reach her. It was still hard for mom to comprehend why Zoe did not apologize to them for not showing up to the party.

I talked to mom about getting some therapy for herself after this, so she could try to move on from this. The situation with Zoe was really taking a toll on her. It was a lot for mom to bear. I saw her pain, and I heard the pain in her voice when we talked on the phone. It was so hard to see and hear mom go through this. She was heartbroken, and I was heartbroken for her. She knew Zoe needed help, but she did not know what to do to help her.

Mom, dad and Zoe were spending a lot of time together again at their house, so these episodes with Zoe being mean and disrespectful to mom continued. Zoe was mean to dad too, but he downplayed it when I would ask him about it. He did not correct her or let her know that she was wrong for the way that she talked to him. And, I'm not sure why. But, what I do know is, her behavior became a way of life.

During this time, I witnessed one of her episodes with dad. He wanted to drive her car to run an errand to pick up something for dinner, and she went off on him and started screaming at him. She did not want him to drive her car and she was not quiet about it. Mom said: "she treats us like that, but she lives off of us." Mom and dad did a lot for Zoe, if she needed anything they were there for her. Which is why it hurt so much to see the way she treated them. Mom and dad would do anything for anyone and they did not deserve to be treated like that. Mom told me Zoe was helping her by taking her to her therapy sessions at the time, but Zoe's biggest concern was what they were having for dinner on a daily basis. What they were having for dinner was always on Zoe's mind, according to mom. It was as if they had to make sure that Zoe had a meal to eat, instead of it being the opposite way around.

While mom continued to try to get Zoe to open up and talk about her behavior toward them, Zoe would tell mom that she was nagging her, so nothing ever came out of it. Mom was diagnosed with dementia during the same time she was dealing with all of this stress from Zoe. Mom tried to work through all of this the best way she knew how, but Zoe's disrespect for mom broke her spirit. Mom endured this lack of respect from Zoe for many years.

Surviving Dysfunction:
It's Not Normal But My Reality
CHAPTER 8

I mentioned earlier about a recent episode with Zoe that I want to touch upon. It was the day after a very close relative's home going, my husband's brother, and my heart was still heavy. Mom was sick, I went to visit her, and Zoe came to visit her that day too. Interestingly enough, she called me first to see if I was there. The doctor had ordered a test for mom, and I had the task of making sure that she drank as much of the contrast as she could tolerate. Once that was done, I decided that I was exhausted and asked Zoe if she could order mom's dinner before she left. Zoe started dishing out her excuses again and said she had to leave too. Mom asked me what was wrong, and I told her, "Nothing, some things never change." I guess mom could see the frustration on my face. Well, what I said offended Zoe, but it was the truth. The truth hurts. One of the reasons why she did not want to stay was because she had ordered her dinner the day before. Really?

Remember, in her mind she is helping me, not her mother. I know, it is not normal, but my normal.

She had all kinds of excuses. I admit it, I lost it and let her know how insensitive she was since my family and I were grieving, and I just wanted to go home and relax. I also let her know that she did not do anything for mom and that she didn't do much for my parents but give them lots of heartache; especially as it relates to mom.

I asked Zoe to calm down given the fact that mom was frail, but she refused repeatedly. She kept trying to get eye contact with mom and was trying to get mom to take sides as if we were little kids. Finally, I had enough and called the nurses for some assistance. I felt like she was a hazard to mom's health, and I wanted her to stop. She could not even bring herself to calm down given the situation. She had to have the last word. There it was. That competition thing again, on full display. I know it's not normal, but it's my reality.

The good thing is, mom had no recollection of this due to her memory loss. On the other hand, I did remember it, and it brought it all back to me how her behavioral issues have affected me for so many years and compelled me to tell my story.

Surviving Dysfunction:
It's Not Normal But My Reality
CHAPTER 9

As mom's memory loss progressed, I noticed that she was slowly starting to forget all of the pain that Zoe had caused her over the years. She was no longer sitting around crying about the hurt and the pain she felt because of Zoe. I guess that was one good thing about her dementia. She no longer remembered all of the pain from the missed holidays and missed birthday dinners, or the pain of not being able to reach Zoe when she knew she was struggling, and needed help.

The dementia had started to overshadow the pain from Zoe. Mom was no longer depressed about Zoe. Mom's dementia was slowly making all of the bad memories fade away. While she labeled Zoe as always being "different", that is where it stopped. No more tears. No more stress. No more heartache.

Surviving Dysfunction

They say dementia can be both a blessing and a curse. In mom's case, I guess this was the blessing because she did not deserve to be treated that way.

Surviving Dysfunction:
It's Not Normal But My Reality
CHAPTER 10

I am glad mom's dementia was slowly taking away the pain from Zoe, and it no longer weighed heavy on her mind. Watching her living with dementia has been hard. At times, she does seem distant, but my family and I do our best to try to keep her engaged. We are happy she is still here and do whatever we can to keep her happy.

I recently read a quote that you are only as happy as your least happy child is. I think that quote is quite fitting here. Zoe blamed mom for many things that went wrong in her life. She never took responsibility for her own mishaps. She never apologized for the hurt that she caused mom or to anyone else in the family. The way that Zoe dealt with it, was to keep her distance after one of her episodes, which could be several months, and to put the blame on us. This was her pity party mode. Then slowly she would make her way back to the family; only for it to happen all over again, by way of another episode. It was never Zoe's fault. She was always the victim, and she is still playing the victim. When we do come together for whatever reason, Zoe always has to bring someone along with her or tries to have someone there, as she says, to be on her side.

It is always about Zoe having things done her way! She is still very much in denial. The only difference is, it no longer affects mom. I do not tell mom what Zoe says or does to hurt anyone in the family anymore. Why bother? Mom's mind is at peace with all of the hurt from Zoe, and that is how I want it to remain.

Surviving Dysfunction:

It's Not Normal But My Reality

CHAPTER 11

It took me some time, but I did learn to move on from all of the deceit and betrayal over the years from Zoe. Do I wish things were different and that my family and I did not have to go through this? Of course I do. Do I wish mom and dad had gotten Zoe help when they first realized she was "different?" (that's their word not mine). Yes, I do. Do I wish Zoe didn't feel like everything is a competition between us? Of course I do. However, things happen for a reason, for which we have no control over. And to that I say, if you have a friend or family member with a long history of behavioral issues or depression, reach out to them if they are ready to get help. But, if they are in denial, there's not much you can do but educate yourself on this subject and let them know you are there for them when they are ready to get help. Get on with your life and do your research on mental illness, and realize that it is not you or anything that you did. It took me a while to get to that point, and I learned that this situation was bigger than me, and that it was not just a "sibling" thing.

I feel like mental illness played a major role in my family's dysfunction. And, to address my question in Chapter 1, it's all three things mentioned: sibling rivalry, family drama, and mental illness all rolled into one. We were dealing with a mental disorder in the family and did not even know it. But, reality kicked in eventually, and I realized it was something much bigger than me or any of us. And, there was nothing we could do about it but move on since Zoe never addressed her behavior and all of the hurt she caused.

Surviving Dysfunction:

It's Not Normal But My Reality

CHAPTER 12

With mental illness in the forefront right now, since we are all living through a pandemic, we are all feeling some anxiety from time to time. It's quite depressing that we can't get together with family anymore, and we are all cooped up in the house right now. We are a hugging family, so this is tough for me and my family. My family and I are doing whatever we can to exercise and get fresh air on a regular basis, so we do not get depressed during these tough times.

I know the signs of depression after living through this with my family, and will do all that I can to get help for my family if they need it and there won't be any stigma attached to it. I would rather see my family members live a happy normal life, even if that includes therapy and taking medication.

I really wish Zoe had gotten some counseling earlier in life due to her low self-esteem and her feeling as if she was always in a competition with me. Those feelings were not normal, but became normal to her as time went on. And, ultimately, those feelings that were deeply rooted in Zoe rose to the surface and became our reality. It did not have to be this way, but it is what it is. We all have to deal with things in life. Things do not always go as planned, and I accepted that and chose to find purpose in my situation, and move on! It was my faith that got me through this, and I am sharing my story in hopes of helping someone else.

I know things can look different from the outside looking in. And, it's very easy for people to say, "well that's between you and her." Or, "y'all need to work it out because you are family." Family or not, it is not easy once those feelings have been allowed to fester and harden over the years, as it has with Zoe. And, when there are no lines of communication, as it relates to sitting down and really talking things out, you have no clue. So, please do not judge. What you can do is listen. Listening is a very powerful tool.

Surviving Dysfunction:

It's Not Normal But My Reality

CONCLUSION

I really hope this book has helped you in some way to know the signs of depression and to be able to help your loved ones and friends when they need it or *if* they want it. And, I can't stress this enough, if your loved one is not ready to get help or are in denial about their behavioral issues, please take care of yourself in the meantime. Take a step back, focus on you, and know that it is not anything that you did. Know that it is something much bigger than you have control over.

As mentioned before, we are living through some very difficult times and we need each other to get through this. I challenge you to check in on your family members or friends. Don't text them, call them and let them know that you are thinking of them and that you care. If your children live with you, and they are spending a lot of time in their bedrooms alone, go into their rooms and talk to them. Ask them how they are doing and if they need anything. If they do not look you in the eye, they might be struggling. Give them a hug. They may need a hug but do not know how to ask for it. Take the first step, and reach out to someone you love today who you think may be struggling with depression or low self-esteem.

Please remember that life is short, so *choose* to be happy. Keep the faith and know that God is in control. Keep smiling, because it confuses your enemies!

As for me, I know that I am loved and I know that my life has purpose. I know my worth, and no one can diminish that.

National Alliance on Mental Illness
www.nami.org
1-800-950-6264

www.ingramcontent.com/pod-product-compliance
Lightning Source LLC
Chambersburg PA
CBHW071416290426
44108CB00014B/1854